Steve Irwin

W. M. Anderson

CAMBRIDGE
UNIVERSITY PRESS

PUBLISHED BY THE PRESS SYNDICATE OF THE UNIVERSITY OF CAMBRIDGE
The Pitt Building, Trumpington Street, Cambridge, United Kingdom

CAMBRIDGE UNIVERSITY PRESS
The Edinburgh Building, Cambridge CB2 2RU, UK
40 West 20th Street, New York, NY 10011–4211, USA
477 Williamstown Road, Port Melbourne 3207, Australia
Ruiz de Alarcón 13, 28014 Madrid, Spain
Dock House, The Waterfront, Cape Town 8001, South Africa

http://www.cambridge.edu.au

First published in 2003

Printed in Australia by Hyde Park Press

Typeface Plantin Light 14/17 pt *System* QuarkXPress® [PC]

National Library of Australia Cataloguing in Publication data
    Anderson, Wendy.
    Steve Irwin.
    For teenagers with reading ages below eleven.
    ISBN 0 521 53839 4.
    1. Irwin, Steve. 2. Herpetologists — Australia —
    Biography. I. Title. (Series: Livewire real lives).
597.9092

ISBN 0 521 53839 4 paperback

Acknowledgements:
Photographs: Cover photo courtesy of News Ltd.
All other images kindly supplied with the permission
of Australia Zoo Pty Ltd and Steve and Terri Irwin.

Contents

		Page
1	'By Crikey'	1
2	Growing Up with Snakes	3
3	A Zoo at Beerwah	9
4	'Jumping Crocs'	12
5	Mr and Mrs Crocodile Hunter	21

Steve is feeding an Australian Saltwater Crocodile at Australia Zoo.

1 'By Crikey'

He says funny things. He gets excited about wild animals. His eyes stick out when he talks. He jumps around in his green shorts. He gets so excited that he looks like he could jump right out of his green shorts.

There is a talking doll of him. He has been on television shows and is in the movie *Dr. Doolittle 2* with Eddie Murphy.

He was in the cartoon show called 'South Park'. He was even a puppet on 'Sesame Street'. It is Steve Irwin, an amazing Australian.

Steve Irwin is 'The Crocodile Hunter'. But he does not hunt crocodiles with guns. He hunts them with cameras.

Crocodiles are not ugly monsters. They are amazing animals. That's what Steve Irwin thinks. Steve loves all animals. He wants us to love them too.

Steve works to save animals all over the planet. He has told us about sea snakes, elephants, camels, otters, turtles, spiders, monkeys, even wild pigs. And he has been excited about all of them. He has been bitten by lots of them too!

Steve is even making a 'Crocodile Hunter' cartoon series. It is not just for fun. He also wants to tell very young kids about animals.

Steve says, 'I believe that education is all about being excited. If we can get people excited about animals, then by crikey, it makes it a heck of a lot easier to save them'.

2   Growing Up with Snakes

Stephen Robert Irwin (Steve) was born in 1962.

His father Robert (Bob) was a plumber. His
mother Lynette (Lyn) was a nurse. Steve has
two sisters. They are called Joy and Mandy.
The Irwin family lived in Essendon. Essendon
is in Melbourne, Australia.

Bob and Lyn Irwin loved animals. Not just cats
and dogs, they also loved wild animals. They took
their children camping. The family would watch
the wildlife. They liked to learn about Australian
native animals. Australian native animals are
animals that live in the bush.

Bob knew all about reptiles. He cared about them too. Snakes, lizards, turtles and crocodiles are reptiles. Bob had reptiles for pets. Steve grew up in a house full of snakes.

Bob and Lyn Irwin with a six metre long python. They are helping it take off extra skin.

Bob took Steve with him on trips to the bush. They hunted for reptiles. Bob would catch snakes and lizards. He would catch a deadly snake in his bare hands. He would grab the snake behind the head. Or he would grab its tail and hold the snake away from him. Then Bob would put the live snake into a bag to take it home.

Steve watched his dad. He wanted to be just like him. He wanted to do what Bob did. Bob was his hero.

Steve wanted a snake of his own. He got one for his sixth birthday. It was a 2.6 metre python. Steve called him 'Fred'.

Pythons do not bite. They crush the things they kill. They also like to eat live animals. Steve would catch mice for Fred to eat.

One day, Steve made a big mistake. He found a brown snake. Brown snakes are the second most deadly of all snakes in the world. Steve tried to catch the snake. He put his foot on it. Then he called his dad to come and help. But Steve did not put his foot near its head. He put his foot in the middle of the snake.

Bob saw the angry snake. He knew it was about to bite Steve. Bob pushed Steve. He shouted at him. He told Steve he was stupid. He had told him never to touch a brown snake. Steve was very upset. He wanted to run away. He was only seven.

Steve loved to play sport. He went to cricket by bus. One day he did not bat well. Then, he had to wait around.

Steve was bored. He started to look for lizards. What he found was a red-bellied black snake.

Steve caught the deadly snake by the tail. He did not have a bag to put it in. So he put the snake in an Esky. It was the bus driver's Esky.

That day Steve filled the Esky with red-bellied black snakes. He wanted to take them home for his dad. The bus driver was really angry. So was Steve's dad.

Bob outside the Beerwah Reptile Park.

3   A Zoo at Beerwah

In 1970, the Irwin family moved to Queensland. Bob and Lyn bought some land at Beerwah. Beerwah is near the Glasshouse Mountains in Queensland. It is north of Brisbane.

The Irwins wanted to teach people about reptiles and Australian wildlife. They wanted their own little zoo. So they set up the Beerwah Reptile Park.

Bob and Steve went all over Australia to catch reptiles. Steve liked these trips better than school. He says he had a really big sandpit to play in – Central Australia!

Lyn was a nurse. That was lucky for Steve. He was always hurting himself. Lyn also looked after animals, such as kangaroos that were hit by cars, possums that were hurt on power lines and birds that were caught by cats.

Lyn took care of the hurt animals or their babies. Most of them went back into the bush. But some animals stayed in the park.

The Irwins were proud of their wildlife park. They loved all the animals. They knew them all too. Bob and Steve had caught the reptiles. Lyn had saved the other animals.

By 1980, they had to change the name of the park. There were many kinds of animals, not just reptiles. They called it the Queensland Reptile and Fauna Park. 'Fauna' means all sorts of animals.

In 1991, Bob and Lyn gave up work. Steve took over the wildlife park. It grew bigger. It is now called Australia Zoo. It has more than 550 animals from all over the world. There are over 100 crocodiles.

About 250 people now work at Australia Zoo. Steve plans to spend $40 million over the next 15–20 years to make it bigger and better.

4 'Jumping Crocs'

Crocodiles have not changed for 160 million years. They are living dinosaurs. Crocodiles can live to be 100 years old. They are the biggest reptiles on Earth.

'Crocodiles should be seen as the king of all Australian animals,' says Steve.

There are two sorts of crocodiles in Australia. There are freshwater and saltwater crocodiles.

Saltwater crocodiles are also called 'salties'. They can grow to six metres long. They can weigh as much as 1000 kilograms. A saltwater crocodile can grab an animal as big as a cow in its strong mouth.

Freshwater crocodiles are called 'freshies'. They are not as big. They only eat small things.

Crocodiles kill a big animal in a special way. First, they grab the animal and bite it hard. Then they shake it. Then they do a death roll. A death roll is when the crocodile rolls around in the water. Crocodiles drown the animals. Big crocodiles can stay under water for more than an hour.

People used to shoot crocodiles. They even blew them up with dynamite. The number of crocodiles in Australia got very low. So, in 1963, freshwater crocodiles became protected animals. Protected means that no one can kill them. Saltwater crocodiles have been protected since 1974.

Crocodiles that live close to people have to be moved. Crocodiles that are a problem to humans are called 'rogue' crocodiles. Rogue crocodiles are trapped. Then they are taken further away and let go. If there is no safe place, they end up in parks like Australia Zoo.

Bob Irwin worked with rogue crocodiles in the 1970s. He took Steve with him. He showed Steve how to catch live crocodiles. It is called 'jumping a croc'.

Bob and Steve went out in a boat at night. Bob was in the front of the boat. Steve was at the back. Steve was in charge of the motor.

They shone spotlights over the water. The light shines back off a crocodile's eyes. The crocodile's eyes look like red dots in the dark. This is called 'eye-shine'. You can tell how big the crocodile is by the eye-shine. If the red spots are far apart, it is a big crocodile. If the spots are close, it is a small crocodile.

Bob and Steve found a crocodile resting on the mud. Steve moved the boat close to the animal. Bob put his spotlight down. Steve held his light up high. Then Bob jumped off the boat onto the crocodile.

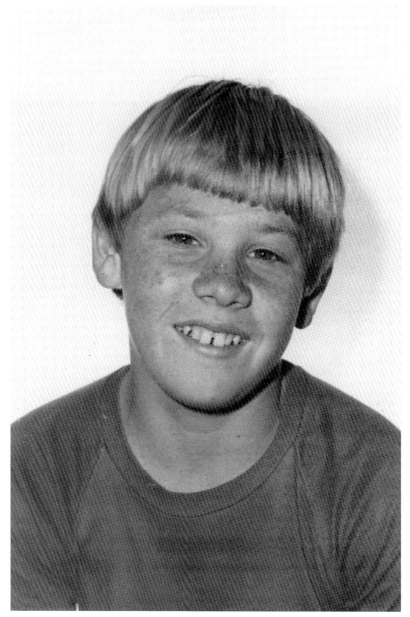

Steve was only nine years old when he jumped his first croc.

Bob held the crocodile around the neck. He grabbed its tail with his legs. When the croc got tired, Bob rolled it into the boat. Then it was Steve's job to lie on the croc in the boat to hold it down. Bob got back in the boat. He put a blindfold over the crocodile's eyes. This helps to keep it quiet. Then he put the croc in a bag.

One night they went to catch some freshies. The crocodiles had to be moved from a farm. Bob and Steve came across a one-metre crocodile. This time, Bob moved to the back of the boat. It was Steve's turn to jump the croc.

Steve was nine years old. He was thrilled. He has been jumping crocodiles ever since.

In the 1980s, Steve trapped rogue crocodiles in North Queensland. He used nets, ropes and a small boat. Steve worked and lived alone for months on end.

His best friend was his dog Chilli. Chilli died after she got shot. Steve still does not like to talk about it.

Steve with a rogue saltwater crocodile at Cattle Creek. He trapped it with the net. The ropes keep its mouth shut.

The biggest crocodile Steve ever trapped on his own was Acco. Acco had been killing cattle from local farms for over 20 years. It would be only a matter of time before Acco was shot by a farmer. Steve tracked the big black saltwater crocodile for more than a year. Acco was smart. And he was far too big to jump.

One day, Acco got stuck in a net trap. When Acco did his death roll, he ended up in the boat. He was trapped in there by the ropes.

The tide was coming in. The boat was sinking. Steve knew Acco could drown. He needed help. So Steve went off to get some farmers to help him. They moved the crocodile with a tractor.

Acco is nearly five metres long. He weighs 1000 kilograms. Just his head weighs the same as all of Steve. Acco now lives at Australia Zoo.

Acco does not look very happy to see Steve.

5 Mr and Mrs Crocodile Hunter

1991 was a big year for Steve Irwin. Bob and Lyn gave him Australia Zoo. Steve was very happy to take over as the boss.

In October 1991, he met Terri Raines. She is now his wife. She is also the one who takes care of the money. Steve and Terri joke that he is Tarzan and she is Jane. Steve is the wild one. Terri is the sensible one.

Terri Raines comes from Oregon in America. Her dad worked around the country. He would bring home animals that were hurt on the road. Terri took care of them. She worked hard. She was good with money. Terri bought a house when she was only 18. She was a boss at 20.

Terri also worked to take care of American wildlife. She loved native cats best. Terri had 15 cougars. She also worked for a vet.

Terri came to Australia for a holiday. She was also keen to see some of the wildlife. She saw a crocodile show at Australia Zoo. She fell in love with the man working with the big reptiles. She could see how much he cared about crocodiles. It was Steve.

She asked him if he had a girlfriend. Steve said yes. He asked Terri if she wanted to meet her. Then Steve called over his dog Sui. Terri still loves the way Steve makes her laugh.

Terri with Malina. Malina was one of Terri's cougar friends in America.

Steve and Terri got married in Oregon in June 1992. They hate to be apart. They had a baby girl in July 1998. Her name is Bindi-Sue.

Steve chose 'Bindi'. It is an Aboriginal word for 'girl'. It is also the name of one of Steve's crocodiles. Terri chose 'Sue' because of Steve's dog – Sui.

Even Bindi-Sue works at Australia Zoo. She loves to be part of the snake shows. Bindi-Sue likes to kiss snakes. She is just like her dad and her grandfather.

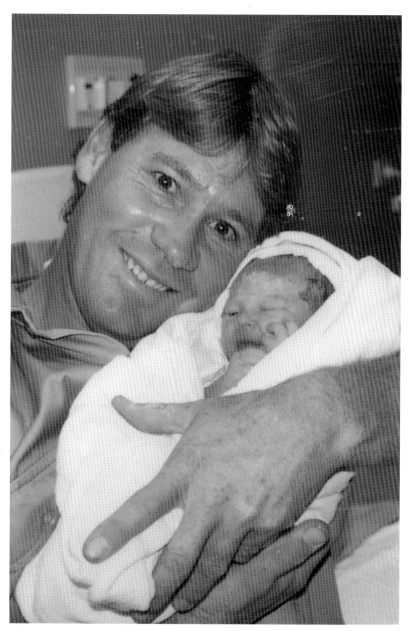

Steve with baby Bindi Sue. She had just been born. Steve loves being a dad.

In the same year that Steve and Terri met, a man was making a television show at Australia Zoo. It was not about Steve. But the man saw Steve doing a crocodile show for the crowd. He asked Steve if he wanted to make a television show. Steve said, 'Why not?' They made 'The Crocodile Hunter'. People loved it. They wanted to see more.

Steve and Terri got a call about a crocodile that needed help. They were on their honeymoon at the time. They went off to save the animal. The camera crew went with them.

Steve and Terri have now made over 100 wildlife shows. More than 200 million people watch Steve and Terri on television.

In 2000, Steve's mum Lyn died in a car crash. Steve and Terri were in the planning stages of making a feature film. Lyn would have been proud of Steve's movie.

The Crocodile Hunter: Collision Course cost $23 million to make. It is like two movies in one. It is an action story. It is also about looking after wild animals. Steve says that every cent earned from the movie has gone towards saving wildlife.

The Irwins plan to keep making films and television shows. As Terri says, 'People tune in because they want to see this guy die or get badly hurt. And instead they get a message about wildlife, and they get to see a guy who says, "Isn't this rattlesnake beautiful?" Who else says that?'

Only the amazing Steve Irwin.